REALITY TV IS A BIG DEAL THESE DAYS.

BUT WHAT HAPPENS WHEN REALITY TV GOES TOO FAR?

TAKEN TO EXTREMES, IT'S A CONCEPT THAT BOTH HORRIFIES AND FASCINATES US.

THAT FASCINATION IS A DRIVING FORCE BEHIND THE SUCCESS OF *SUZANNE COLLINS*' BEST-SELLING BOOK SERIES...

THE HUNGER GAMES.

MOST READERS KNOW VERY LITTLE ABOUT THE WOMAN BEHIND THE WORDS.

A FAMOUSLY PRIVATE PERSON, SUZANNE COLLINS DOESN'T SHARE MUCH ABOUT HER CHILDHOOD.

BUT GROWING UP DURING THE VIETNAM WAR WOULD PROVE INSTRUMENTAL IN FORMING THE BOOK

AND WHEN HE RETURNED, HE WASN'T AFRAID TO TELL HIS YOUNG DAUGHTER REAL-LIFE STORES ABOUT THE WAR.

"if you went to a battlefield with him you didn't just stand there. You would hear what led up to this war and to this particular battle, what transpired there, and what the fallout was. it wasn't like, 'There's a field.' it would be, 'Here's a story.'"

THESE STORIES WOULD LATER SERVE AS INSPIRATION FOR MANY ELEMENTS IN HER BEST-SELLING TRILOGY, THE HUNGER GAMES

THERE, SHE GOT HER MFA IN DRAMATIC WRITING FROM NEW YORK UNIVERSITY.

IN 1991, COLLINS BEGAN HER CAREER IN CHILDREN'S TELEVISION.

New Character

COLLINS WORKED HARD AND BECAME AN IMPORTANT PART OF THE WRITING TEAM AT THE KIDS' NETWORK, *NICKELODEON.* SHE MADE HER MARK ON SOME OF THE NETWORK'S BIGGEST SHOWS OF THE 1990'S & EARLY 2000'S: *"CLARISSA EXPLAINS IT ALL"*, *"THE MYSTERY FILES OF SHELBY WOO"*, *"LITTLE BEAR"*, *"OSWALD."*

Vol. 225

Vol. 238

00

Cliffor

Clifford's

iffor PUPPY

PUPPY DAYS

PY D

FROM THERE, SHE BECAME THE HEAD WRITER FOR SCHOLASTIC'S TV SHOW, *"CLIFFORD'S PUPPY DAYS."*

AND IN 2003, SHE WAS NOMINATED BY THE WRITER'S GUILD OF AMERICA FOR CO-WRITING THE CHRISTMAS SPECIAL, "SANTA BABY."

COLLINS HAD BECOME A SUCCESS IN THE WORLD OF CHILDREN'S TELEVISION ...

BUT A CHANCE MEETING WOULD SOON CHANGE THINGS DRAMATICALLY FOR HER.

WHILE WORKING ON THE KIDS CW SHOW *"GENERATION O!"* IN 2000-2001, COLLINS MET CHILDREN'S AUTHOR JAMES PROIMOS.

HE'S THE ONE WHO FIRST SUGGESTED SHE TRY HER HAND AT WRITING BOOKS FOR CHILDREN.

THE IDEA TOOK SEED ...

COLLINS SOON FOUND HERSELF CONTEMPLATING ONE OF THE MOST BELOVED CHILDREN'S STORIES OF ALL TIME ...

ALICE IN WONDERLAND.

COLLINS BEGAN THINKING ABOUT THE BOOK'S PASTORAL SETTING...

...AND HOW STRANGE IT MUST SEEM TO MODERN KIDS WHO GROW UP IN URBAN SETTINGS.

SHE TRADED A MANHOLE FOR A RABBIT HOLE AND THUS, THE UNDERLAND CHRONICLES WAS BORN, A MAGICAL LAND THRIVING BENEATH THE STREETS OF MANHATTAN.

"I liked the fact that this world was teeming under New York City and nobody was aware of it. That you could be going along preoccupied with your own problems and then *whoosh!*"

FROM 2003-2007, COLLINS WROTE FIVE BOOKS IN THE UNDERLAND CHRONICLES, A SERIES FOR MIDDLE GRADE READERS.

THOUGH WRITTEN FOR KIDS, THE BOOKS TOUCHED ON HEAVY SUBJECTS: DEATH, VIOLENCE, GENOCIDE, BIOLOGICAL WARFARE.

COLLINS BELIEVED HER YOUNG AUDIENCE WAS CAPABLE OF UNDERSTANDING SUCH MATURE THEMES.

"I felt that if my audience came with me from the beginning of that series, they would be able to understand that in context."

IT WAS A CONCEPT THAT WOULD STICK WITH HER FOR HER BIGGEST PROJECT YET.

IT WAS WHILE SHE WAS WORKING ON BOOKS FOR YOUNGER READERS, WHEN A DARKER INSPIRATION CAME TO COLLINS ...

IT STARTED ONE NIGHT AS COLLINS WAS CHANNEL-SURFING.

3 SOLDIERS KILLED, FIGHTING CONTINUES

AS SHE FLIPPED BETWEEN NEWS COVERAGE OF WAR AND A REALITY PROGRAM, THE LINES BECAME BLURRED ...

WHAT WAS REAL?

WHAT WAS ENTERTAINMENT?

"There's this potential for desensitizing the audience so that when they see real tragedy playing out on the news, it doesn't have the impact it should. it all just blurs into one program."

"I think it's very important not just for young people, but for adults to make sure they're making the distinction. Because the young soldiers dying in the war in iraq, it's not going to end at the commercial break. it's not something fabricated, it's not a game. it's your life."

THESE THOUGHTS WERE THE BEGINNINGS OF WHAT WOULD LATER BECOME COLLINS' MOST POPULAR WORK TO DATE ...

THE HUNGER GAMES.

IN 2006, COLLINS SIGNED A SIX-FIGURE, THREE-BOOK DEAL WITH SCHOLASTIC AND BEGAN WORK ON THE FIRST PART OF HER EPIC TRILOGY.

FOR MORE INSPIRATION, SHE TURNED TO THE WAR STORIES HER FATHER TOLD HER WHEN SHE WAS A CHILD.

Ancient Greece

IN ANCIENT TIMES, THE CITY OF **ATHENS** WAGED WAR ON THE CITY OF **CRETE**.

BUT ATHENS LOST THE WAR, AND AS RETRIBUTION, **KING MINOS** OF CRETE MADE THE AT HENEANS PAY A HORRIBLE PRICE.

HE FORCED THE CITY TO SEND **SEVEN BOYS** AND **SEVEN GIRLS** AS TRIBUTES TO CRETE.

THERE, THE CHILDREN WOULD BE DEVOURED BY THE **MINOTAUR** AS RETRIBUTION FOR THE ATHENEANS' FAILED WAR.

THE PEOPLE OF ATHENS GRIEVED FOR THEIR LOST CHILDREN, AS THIS PATTERN CONTINUED FOR **MANY YEARS** … UNTIL **THESEUS** CAME ALONG, AND TOOK THE PLACE OF ONE OF THE SEVEN BOYS.

WHEN THESEUS ARRIVED IN CRETE WITH THE OTHER **TRIBUTES**, THE DAUGHTER OF KING MINOS FELL IN LOVE WITH HIM – AND SHARED WITH HIM SECRETS TO HELP HIM **DEFEAT** THE MINOTAUR.

USING HER SECRETS, THESEUS SLAYED THE MINOTAUR AND ESCAPED WITH THE OTHER TRIBUTES BACK TO ATHENS.

THOUGH THERE IS NO MINOTAUR IN THE HUNGER GAMES, COLLINS USED THE MYTH AS THE FOUNDATION FOR HER BOOKS' DYSTOPIAN WORLD OF PANEM.

A WORLD WHERE THE GOVERN-MENT FORCES EACH OF THE COUNTRY'S 12 DISTRICTS TO SEND CHILDREN AS TRIBUTES, TO FIGHT TO THE DEATH FOR TELEVISED ENTERTAINMENT.

WITH AN INITIAL PRINTING OF 200,000, THE HUNGER GAMES DEBUTED TO CRITICAL PRAISE AND WAS AN INSTANT *NEW YORK TIMES* BEST SELLER.

AND MOVIE PRODUCERS QUICKLY SNAPPED UP THE FILM RIGHTS.

READERS OF ALL AGES WERE CAPTIVATED BY THE STORY OF 16-YEAR-OLD KATNISS EVERDEEN AND THE HORRORS OF COLLINS' VISION OF A FUTURISTIC, DYSTOPIAN UNITED STATES.

COLLINS' POPULARITY ONLY GREW WITH THE RELEASE OF THE SECOND BOOK, *CATCHING FIRE*, IN 2009.

FANS ALIGNED THEMSELVES WITH "TEAM PEETA" OR "TEAM GALE" ...

AND FAN SITES BEGAN CROPPING UP ACROSS THE INTERNET.

BY 2010, THE FANDOM HAD ARRIVED AND READERS EAGERLY ANTICIPATED THE RELEASE OF *MOCKINGJAY*, THE THIRD AND FINAL BOOK IN THE *HUNGER GAMES* TRILOGY.

THE MOST DIE-HARD FANS LINED UP FOR HOURS TO BE SOME OF THE FIRST TO GET THEIR HANDS ON THE BOOK. STORES ACROSS THE COUNTRY PLAYED HOST TO MIDNIGHT RELEASE PARTIES, COMPLETE WITH COSTUME CONTESTS AND THEMED GAMES.

MOCKINGJAY WAS A SUCCESS.

IN THE MIDST OF ALL THE MOCKINGJAY FRENZY, FANS GOT HIT WITH ANOTHER DOSE OF GOOD NEWS ...

A MOVIE VERSION WAS ON THE WAY.

COLLINS HERSELF PENNED THE FIRST DRAFT OF THE SCREENPLAY, AND *LIONSGATE* HIRED *GARY ROSS* TO DIRECT.

THE COVETED ROLE OF KATNISS WAS GIVEN TO OSCAR-NOMINATED ACTRESS *JENNIFER LAWRENCE*.

AND AS HER POTENTIAL PARAMOURS - JOSH HUTCHERSON WAS CAST AS PEETA, AND LIAM HEMSWORTH WAS CAST AS GALE.

COMING SOON!

ITH THE FILM SLATED OR RELEASE IN MARCH 012, FANS ARE EAGERLY NTICIPATING WHAT IT WILL E LIKE TO SEE THEIR ELOVED STORY TOLD ON HE BIG SCREEN.

BUT THE SPOTLIGHT CLEARLY LOVES HER - WITH THE FANDOM FOR THE *HUNGER GAMES* ONLY CONTINUING TO GROW AS WORK ON THE MOVIE MOVES FORWARD.

Hunger Games casting rumor

Hunger Games movie release date announced

Who should play Katniss in The Hunger Games?

Exclusive: Hunger Games director Gary Ross

REGARDLESS OF HOW THE MOVIE IS RECEIVED, COLLINS HAS NOTHING TO WORRY ABOUT.

WHETHER SHE'S GREETING FANS AT PACKED BOOK EVENTS ...

OR CURLED UP AT HOME WITH HER FAMILY IN CONNECTICUT ...

COLLINS HAS SECURED HER ROLE IN POPULAR CULTURE FOR YEARS TO COME.

END